# WHAT'S
## *in a*
# TITLE?

DR. VALERIE K. BROWN

CREATION HOUSE
A STRANG COMPANY

WHAT'S IN A TITLE? by Valerie K. Brown
Published by Creation House
A Strang Company
600 Rinehart Road
Lake Mary, Florida 32746
www.creationhouse.com

Unless otherwise noted, all Scripture quotations are from
the Holy Bible, New Living Translation, copyright © 1996.
Used by permission of Tyndale House Publishers, Inc.,
Wheaton, IL 60189. All rights reserved.

Cover design by Terry Clifton

Library of Congress Control Number: 2005930406
International Standard Book Number: 1-59185-880-1

First Edition

05 06 07 08 09 — 987654321
Printed in the United States of America

# ACKNOWLEDGMENTS

I would like to take this opportunity to thank my husband, Rev. Dr. Kim W. Brown, Senior Pastor of Mount Lebanon Missionary Baptist Church, for encouraging me and allowing me to use my gift of administration as Executive Pastor of the church.

I would also like to thank Chilee Holt for all her help and assistance in reading the manuscript and offering constructive editorial changes.

I would also like to thank the hundreds of unnamed individuals and churches who over the years have inspired my writing by challenging me with questions that forced me to not only research the Word of God, but to pray for divine revelation and guidance.

Last, but certainly not least, my thanks always to God who ultimately is the inspiration for me to write for Him for the people. I can never thank God enough for instilling this call upon my life and guiding me each and every step of the way so I can be used as a needed vessel for this venue of kingdom building.

# CONTENTS

# FOREWORD

There are three camps forming within the Christian community with two of these three camps diametrically opposed in their opinions on the usage of titles in the church. One camp maintains the posture that titles should be used in their traditional format restricted to their particular denominational definitions and responsibilities. The other camp is much more liberal, giving way to the usage of titles outside the traditional norm and providing new definitions, roles, and responsibilities for those titles. The first two camps are primarily composed of individuals who currently occupy leadership positions and are justifying their "titles" either through the traditional lens or through the new charismatic lens. The third camp is caught in the middle. This third camp is primarily made up of members of various churches of varying denominations who dared ignite the polarization by asking the question, "How can a Baptist pastor be a bishop? Aren't bishops in the Catholic Church?"

There is a loud cry of excitement and anticipation from those in the third camp now that they are finally beginning to see their questions being raised in a public forum even if no definitive answers have yet come forward that both of the diametrically opposed camps can agree upon. It is the dialogue that will eventually uncover answers or propel the church to its next dimension of leadership structure. Change, rarely if ever, occurs within the confines of obscurity. For such a radical change in the usage of leadership titles as this, it is inevitable that a discussion of this magnitude would come to the forefront of those in positions to address the issue.

In a world (society) where everyone is defined by their material possessions, net worth, and occupation, there are those that believe the church has fallen victim to the usage of titles to bestow power, prestige, and honor to individuals rather than for their functional use. This book invites you to join the conversation as you read each chapter even though it has the propensity to make you uncomfortable and begin to question those in leadership around you with various titles. This book will confirm for some what they have believed all along about the usage of titles. For others, there will be a blatant disagreement with the author. If that happens for some readers (and it will), the book will have accomplished its purpose in opening the dialogue between the pulpit and the pew to address questions the members have been afraid to ask.

As you read, expect to be challenged in your traditional, denominational thinking. Be ready and open, however, for a revelation from God in understanding how titles should be used and for what purposes. Be ready with your pen and paper to write down undoutedly more questions that will arise as you engage the issues of great importance for the church that are discussed in each chapter. Questions such as:

- Does every pastor need a covering or are they simply accountable to God?

- Are the members of a congregation supposed to follow the leadership blindly?

- Does everyone who holds a leadership position need to be a licensed minister of the gospel?

- Are there other types of licenses other than for the gospel ministry?

As you consider these and other questions, the author's desire is that you focus on thinking about the framework from which leadership must operate in order to be the effective and efficient church God would desire in order to achieve its purpose and call not only to the local church but also to the community, region, and nation.

# PREFACE

I t is very easy to become confused about the roles, responsibilities, and associated titles of those in leadership in today's church. The confusion comes in part because of the new trend of using traditional church titles in a nontraditional way. This nontraditional usage of titles entails everything from the elimination of titles all together to some denominations using (or borrowing) titles that were once sacred to other denominations and would never have been used in their ministry context. For example, traditionally, a person could visit a church of any denomination and immediately know by the individual's title what his or her level of authority and leadership responsibilities encompassed. This was true because denominations traditionally carried and used the same titles within their denominations. One example of this is Catholic churches using the title of "bishop" and Baptist churches, not using the title of bishop, but using the

1

title of "pastor." The same was true for other denominations such as Church of God in Christ, Methodists, Episcopalians; they all had titles that were germane to their denomination. There was little, if any, confusion over which denominations used which titles to identify levels of authority within the church.

However, today this has changed in churches. Many churches are breaking away from the traditional operating paradigms of title usage. Under this new operating paradigm, one might find a Baptist "pastor" being called a "bishop." One might also find the marquee of a church identify the church not from a traditional denomination such as Baptist, Methodist, Catholic, etc; but as "nondenominational" or "interdenominational." This new trend of using titles in a nontraditional way has left members confused and asking for clarity and understanding.

Those who are biblically astute readily acknowledge that the Bible does not initiate or advocate any particular denomination. Further research into the Bible also shows no particular denominational governance structure. There are no scriptural references pertaining to a specific denomination. Several references can be found throughout the Bible from which every denomination has taken part of their governance structure and has added their ideas and traditions about church leadership. In light of this, it is quite difficult for any one denomination to say they have it all right. I believe each denomination has part of their leadership models correct while some of it is not biblically grounded.

However years of denominational teachings have embedded certain expectations and values associated with the traditional paradigms. Hundreds of years of operating in a certain paradigm and using certain titles with associated responsibilities created the denominational foundations and beliefs that so many devoted church members believed were the only way in which they could be used. Mintzberg, in his book, *Power In and Around Organizations*, supports this argument by saying that as organizations develop their theology or beliefs, they reinforce themselves over time through the actions taken by the organization. These actions are in turn "infused with value." Therefore... "the precedents, habits, myths, and history of an organization form a common base of tradition which members of the organization share. Over time, this tradition influences behavior, and that behavior in turn reinforces the tradition."[1]

Paul F. Salipante and Karen Golden-Biddle, in *Managing Traditionality and Strategic Change*, make the argument that individuals rely on past behavioral norms to legitimize actions and decisions of current day practices. This is because tradition is a "highly valued source of wisdom." Thus, it becomes difficult to change a practice, policy, or procedure because of the long-lived organizational identity associated with the wisdom of the current status quo. "Traditionality," argues Salipante, "better describes the actual functioning of an organization than does strategic rationality."[2]

It is no wonder then, why there is so much confusion, debate, and dialogue over how and why churches are now changing their operating paradigms in the area of leadership titles and governance structures. Years of tradition have added such value to current operating paradigms that they have become sacred cows.

It is not the intent of this book to speak against anyone's denominational beliefs or teachings. The purpose is to identify the struggle and search for understanding and divine revelation as it relates to the current raging debate over changes in leadership titles and organizational structure. Today titles and their meanings vary across denominational lines. Governance structures have changed dramatically in many denominations from their traditional beginnings. However, the *essence* of leadership and governance structure has not changed; they can be grounded in biblical truths that undergird the foundation for why leadership and governance structure were created. If we can agree on the *essence* of why leadership and governance structure were originally created, we can begin to open a new dialogue from a different perspective that will help answer and address some of the concerns and questions being posed by the confused church member.

In an effort to add to the dialogue and hopefully offer some insight into the debate, I am approaching the topic by framing the question of "Why were leadership and governance structures (and/or titles) created within the church in the first place and what was its initial purpose?" Clearly, in reading the Bible, God's goal was to bring order out of potential chaos. Are we not, therefore, as we struggle to identify an effective operating paradigm, simply trying to ensure that during our "wilderness" experiences here on earth, that we have leaders who are following the legacies of Moses, Joshua, or Joseph who will direct and lead us into our promised land?

## CHAPTER 1

# LEADERSHIP IS A CALLING
# AND A GIFT FROM GOD

Many of you may have read some, or all, the literature on leaders versus managers, or perhaps heard the discussion of whether leaders are born or bred. This book is not an attempt to discuss either of these viewpoints. Instead, it is an effort to research the Word of God and find biblical grounds for understanding leadership for the church of the new millennium. Romans 12:6–8 (emphasis added) reads:

> God has given each of us the ability to do certain things well. So if God has given you the ability to prophesy, speak out when you have faith that God is speaking through you. If your gift is that of serving others, serve them well. If you are a teacher, do a good job of teaching. If your gift is to encourage others, do it! If you have money, share it generously. If God has given you *leadership ability*, take the responsibility seriously.

It easily can be seen from this passage that God will bless some individuals with leadership abilities. Those so blessed are required to "take those responsibilities seriously." Whether God endows you with these abilities at birth or allows you to experience situations and life lessons to produce good leadership traits and skills is beyond the focus of this book. We are focusing on the fact that God is at the center of distributing leadership abilities.

Ephesians 4:11–15 reminds us that God gave the gift(s) of leadership to the church so the members of the church could be equipped to do the work of the kingdom and build up the church. Therefore, church members should always be willing to be under the leadership and authority of those men and women called by God to teach and nourish them so they can grow into spiritual maturity. This is where many in the church have a problem. Never before has there been a society so adverse to authority. We see it everyday in our children refusing to obey their parents, their teachers in school, the police…anyone in an authoritative position. It is no wonder the children behave this way, as it is seen far too often in the parents' behavior as well. Everyone believes they know the best way to operate the church, how to spend the church's money, what to teach the people, what the church should and should not be doing. While it may be true that others may have a better way of doing things; it is literally impossible for the leadership of the church to try to please hundreds of people who have no responsibility or accountability for the outcome of decisions made on behalf of the church. Few want to follow the leadership of the church.

We must stop here and point out that we are not speaking now about the exceptions to the rule. We know there are some in leadership who should not be there and have left a bad taste in the mouth of many members to the extent that many are unwilling to ever follow leadership again and/or question every decision made by the leadership. One bad apple has truly spoiled the barrel. However, excluding this type of leadership which is entirely another discussion, we are focusing on leaders who are truly called of God and are trying to live a life worthy of following as exemplified by the good fruits exhibited from their lifestyle. We know the Bible teaches us that leaders will be judged first and with greater strictness. The leaders of the church are held by God to be accountable for what they teach the people and allow them to do. If we truly believe this, then we must believe that true leaders called of God also know this, and try to make the decisions they believe have been inspired by God for their ministry. They cannot always rely upon the majority of the people agreeing. Leaders must be given the benefit of the doubt, based on their past performances and lifestyle, to be the leader and the latitude to make decisions. One biblical example of this, (and there are many) can be found in Exodus 13: 17–18. This scripture tells of the route the Israelites took when leaving Egypt heading to the promised land. The scripture says that God told Moses not to take the road which runs through the Philistine territory even though it was the shortest route because if they did, they would have to fight and they were not ready to fight the Philistines. There were more than 600,000 people who left Egypt with Moses. With that many people you can imagine how many told Moses he was going the wrong way, taking them the longest way rather than the shortest way. Although they were right from a directional perspective;

they were wrong when considering the maturity of the people to face adversity. One can argue whether or not Moses should have or could have told more than 600,000 people why he was taking the route he was taking; but the reality was, Moses was the leader and knew best as instructed by God. What we must know as the followers is if we truly trust and believe in the leadership to follow their decisions believing they have the best interest of the ministry and the people at heart. I wonder if any people turned around and went the shortest route any way? While the Bible does not speak to that, knowing people, I can imagine some listened to the complainers and went the way they thought was "right." Sometimes you can be right; but wrong. It is not always about being right; but following and trusting the leader.

The apostle Paul reminds us in Galatians 1: 1 that his call to the ministry (as should be for all who answer the call to leadership in the gospel ministry) was from Jesus Christ and not any man or group of human authority. He further reminds us in Galatians 1:10 that the role of the leader is not to be a people pleaser; but to please God.

Therefore no one should accept a position of leadership in the church without much prayer and guidance. Leadership is a major responsibility as people will depend on you for wisdom, knowledge, and skills to lead them. Leadership can be a great honor and blessing bestowed by God to an individual; however, no individual should ever take the responsibility and position for granted nor take advantage of the people because of the authority that comes with the position.

First Thessalonians 5:12–13 reads, "Dear brothers and sisters, honor those who are your leaders in the Lord's work.

They work hard among you and warn you against all that is wrong. Think highly of them and give them your whole-hearted love because of their work. And remember to live peaceably with each other." This scripture reminds us that a gift is a precious commodity and is given out of love. For God so loved the church, He gave the gift of leadership to men and women in whom He has found favor to use in the furtherance of His will. Therefore, we must honor our man or woman of God. To honor them means to show respect. We respect so many other offices of authority; yet we fail to show the same level of respect for our man and woman of God. We will stand and show respect for those in the offices of judges, presidents of countries, and other dignitaries even if we don't agree with their political agendas; yet, we don't show that same respect for the office of pastor.

We take our men and women of God for granted. The spirit of familiarity has taken root and caused us to see this office as everyday and common. I happen to live beside a well-known national award-winning rapper. I see him everyday in his yard doing everyday, normal things like everybody else. To me, it is no big deal to see and talk to him. However, a day does not pass when others think it is a BIG deal just to get a glimpse of him. People will go to extraordinary efforts just to get close to him, to speak to him. People pay lots of money to see him; Christian people. Yet, you could not get the same Christian person to "pay" the pastor for his teaching even though the Bible teaches us in Galatians 6:6 that "those who are taught the word of God should help their teachers by paying them." Why do we place so little value on the teaching of the gospel?

Delivery trucks come everyday with gifts for the famous rapper from those who say they love him. They don't even really know him and this is a person who has done nothing for them personally. The man and woman of God do so much for you personally and spiritually. Why don't we go to extraordinary measures for them? Why don't we shower them with gifts to say we love them? What does this say about our value system?

CHAPTER 2

# WHAT'S IN A TITLE?

Confusion and concern are growing over the issue that titles traditionally used primarily in one denomination are now being used and embraced in denominations that previously did not recognize nor embrace such titles.

One example is the use of the title "bishop." The traditional Baptist denomination does not use this title within its church. Yet many charismatic, nontraditional Baptist churches now embrace and use the title. Even within the Baptist denomination, there are differences to what the title "bishop" represents. In some instances the title is used to indicate the person, normally the traditional pastor, has planted other churches. The pastors of those churches look to him or her as their pastor; hence, the title "bishop."

There are other Baptist churches, however, which use the title in its most simplistic definition. The word bishop simply means "overseer." Some pastors believe that because they

"oversee" their church—not necessarily any other church—
they can also use the term. Many biblical scholars argue the
words "bishop" and "pastor" are interchangeable. To make
matters more confusing, one can inject a new title, "elder,"
that some argue is also interchangeable with bishop and pastor. 1 Timothy 3:1 is an example of this, depending on the
version of the Bible one uses. The New Living Translation
uses these words: "It is a true saying that if someone wants
to be an *elder*, he desires an honorable responsibility." The
King James Version for that same passage reads: "This is a
true saying, If a man desire the office of a *bishop*, he desireth
a good work." This provokes the questions: Are the offices
of *bishop*, *pastor*, or *elder* the same? Does each title carry
the same responsibilities and level of authority? In looking
at some of the churches that now embrace these titles, that
question is not easily answered. For some churches, these
titles are not the same office, nor do they have the same
responsibilities and levels of authority. It becomes even
more muddled when crossing denominational lines.

The title of "minister" further complicates the discussion
of "bishop," "pastor," and "elder" as titles. For who is the
minister? In some cases, the minister is the pastor. However,
the title of minister is sometimes used to also identify those
individuals who have acknowledged a call into the gospel of
preaching. Once one has preached the initial sermon, he or
she is then called a minister.

But are all ministers "preachers"? The answer var-
ies within different churches. Some churches use the title
to identify individuals in leadership positions within the
church such as the minister of music and the minister of
Christian education. These individuals, in most cases, are
not called to preach the gospel and have not preached an

initial sermon. Yet, they carry the title of minister. Other churches teach that everyone in the church is a minister and has a call from God to "minister" in some capacity, and a lot of people carry the title of minister even though they are not leaders in the church.

One now can begin to understand that as people visit different churches and are asked, "Are you a minister?" they are uncertain how to respond for the title "minister" in their context may not mean the same as in other churches.

One can also now see why parishioners are confused. The above discussion focused on the words "bishop," "elder," "minister," and "pastor." Yet there are many words—such as trustees, deacons, and stewards—that no longer carry the generic meaning and common understanding of the title's role, responsibility, and authority that it once carried. It is no wonder parishioners are asking the question, "What's in a title?"

Joyce Meyer a well-known evangelist, answered this question best for the purpose of this discussion. She remarked in one of her television broadcasts that people constantly ask for her title or what she calls herself. They inquire whether she is considered a preacher, pastor, evangelist, elder, bishop, or teacher. She responded that she was a child of God doing whatever God has called her to do for that season. Meyer indicated she did not need a title, and she further stated people desire to label you with a title so they can define your role and limit your leadership and authority. For example, if you are labeled a preacher, then it is acceptable for you to pastor a church, or if you are an evangelist it is only acceptable for you to evangelize. Refusing to be labeled by titles seems to work very well for Meyer as she ministers throughout the world. For, to the outside world, even without a "title," it is clear the call Meyer has on her life in ministry; and she accomplishes this, for the most part, operating outside the church walls and organizational structure. Undoubtedly, behind the doors of Joyce Meyer Ministries, you can believe the employees know her title, role, and authority. The same follows for those operating in ministry within a "church" environment. They need definitive roles, if not common titles, to identify their responsibilities and to establish order.

Every society uses language for a definitive usage of words. However, *Webster's* does a good job of explaining that words can, and do, have different definitions when used in different situations or paradigms. Each church is left to define what each title means in terms of roles, responsibilities, and levels of authority within that church. It must be further understood that the definition or title chosen to be used probably will not have a universal definition, and can be used differently by others. Clearly, the local church is struggling with its own understanding of biblical leadership and order. This is encouraging for the church of the new millennium, which must have an ear toward God and not man-made traditions. This new church is seeking God's heart to bring the church in order for when Jesus comes back, they will be "the Church" without spot or blemish, obedient to the voice of God.

So, what's in a title? Nothing more than what one is given as his or her responsibilities and level of authority. The title you are called is not as important as the assignments and authority given to you. For example, how often have you gone into a local bank and noticed that everyone is a vice president? I have never seen so many vice presidents that cannot approve even a $100 loan! Under normal circumstances in any other institution, a vice-president is considered someone with some decision-making authority and could probably approve an expenditure of the company of some monetary amount. In fact, most vice presidents of companies have at a departmental budget that they must manage of some monetary magnitude. Another example can be found in some companies with administrative assistants. Under normal circumstances, an administrative assistant would not be considered someone of great authority. However, as most of us know, the administrative assistant can carry substantial authority and make decisions in some cases.

I joke all the time that my title can be "chief cook and bottle-washer" as long as my salary does not decrease and my authority and responsibilities do not change. A title does not make the position; the authority, responsibility, and accountability do. Even Paul in 2 Timothy 2:14 reminds us to stop fighting over words, for it only invites godless arguments and foolish discussions.

Whatever titles you finally decide to use within your church, be sure to articulate their meanings to the members. Explain what authority is vested in each title, responsibilities associated with it, the level of accountability, and to whom the individual reports.

## CHAPTER 3

# LEADERS ARE NOT DEFINED BY THEIR TITLES

The cry of the church of the new millennium is not for more preachers, ministers, elders, or bishops. There are more than enough "preachers" to go around. The cry is for leadership—for a leader who will be spiritually mature, who will be desirous of a personal relationship with Jesus Christ, who will teach the people to be spiritually mature, and who will be accountable for his or her actions. Phillip V. Lewis in his book, *Transformational Leadership*, says, "A new wind is blowing across the face of the church. New ways of thinking and new models are needed."[1] Ecclesiastes 10:5–6 reads: "Kings and rulers make a grave mistake if they give foolish people great authority, and if they fail to give people of proven worth their rightful place of dignity."

Lewis and the scripture from Ecclesiastes have embodied the feelings of the church members of the twenty-first century. These members are not locked into traditional paradigms of leadership organizational structures. Structures can change, and new models of leadership are readily being accepted. New ways of thinking are being encouraged. Church members today are not satisfied with filling leadership positions with unqualified individuals. Too many churches have leaders who simply represent the founding families of the church, are individuals who give the most money to the church, or who appear successful in their personal life. Many times churches do not readily seek God first on leadership positions or use the common sense God gave to determine the skills and talents needed to fill a particular position. Church members rarely look for people who bear the fruit of needed skills and talents. Instead, churches far too often put people in leadership who have been nominated and elected through a popularity contest rather than because of their skills and expertise.

The churches that are displaying exceptional growth are not using the traditional leadership models. People joining churches are not overly concerned with structure, but with the ministry going forth. The church members that are staying in traditional churches are questioning their leadership about the religious practices of their church. Churches must stop hiding behind their traditions and respond to the challenges set in place with the questions from their members. Lewis quoted Albert Einstein as saying, "Everything has changed but our ways of thinking, and if these do not change we drift toward unparalleled catastrophe." The church of the new millennium must wake up and realize the world has changed and is continually changing at a rapid pace. The increase in technology, enhanced lifestyles, and our general thinking has necessitated the need for the church to develop new ways of reaching the lost sinner. The church requires transformational leaders who are people of vision, equipped and inspired to lead, and willing to be transformed by God and not by man or his inspired traditions, according to Lewis.

What model of leadership, then, does the church of the twenty-first century need to follow? The answer is probably as complex as the answer to the earlier question regarding title distinctions. There is no one correct model of leadership. However, what can be discerned for leadership in the twenty-first century church are the *types* of leaders that are needed and the roles and responsibilities each needs to fulfill. In addition, one must biblically ground the reasons for why leadership and governance structures were created originally. I believe there were three basic principles or essential elements for the establishment of leadership governance structure. They are:

## Essential Elements

1. Identifying individuals who have accepted their call by God to leadership

   - "So, dear brothers and sisters, work hard to prove that you really are among those God has called and chosen. Doing this, you will never stumble or fall away" (2 Pet. 1:10).

   - "If God has given you leadership ability, take the responsibility seriously…" (Rom. 12:8).

2. Empowering those individuals so the work of God can go forth in the kingdom through those individuals and through the local church

- "But find some capable, honest men who fear
  God and hate bribes. Appoint them as judges
  over groups of one thousand, one hundred,
  fifty, and ten" (Exod. 18:21).

3. Ensuring the leaders be held accountable for their
   actions

   - "By traveling together we will guard against
     any suspicion, for we are anxious that no
     one should find fault with the way we are
     handling this generous gift. We are careful
     to be honorable before the Lord, but we also
     want everyone else to know we are honor-
     able" (2 Cor. 8:20–21).

   - "It isn't my responsibility to judge outsid-
     ers, but it certainly is your job to judge those
     inside the church who are sinning in these
     ways" (1 Cor. 5:12).

Now, what types of leaders are needed for the church of
today? Spiritually mature leaders are needed who can:

1. Preach, teach, and cast vision

2. Manage the day-to-day administrative task of run-
   ning a church

3. Minister to the congregational needs of the adults

4. Minister to the congregational needs of the youth/
   young adults

5. Empower the members so they can become
   spiritually mature, evangelize for Christ, and

develop a close personal relationship with Christ themselves

These types of leadership positions are not innovative; yet, who should fill these positions is the point of controversy. More than twenty years ago in the traditional Baptist churches, it was assumed the pastor was responsible to do everything except play the music, even though there were some who played the music or took the liberty to sing quite often. The pastor was responsible for all these functions even though he may not have been trained or have had the experience to adequately fulfill them. Within the past twenty years or so, churches realized the pastors could not do everything, so positions were filled with licensed preachers called to gospel ministry. Licensed preachers were employed as ministers of music, youth ministers, administrators, and as ministers of Christian education. Even with these changes in positions, many churches still did not find ministry operating at an efficient and effective level of acceptability. Something was still missing from the essential elements. Eventually, someone asked the question: Why are only licensed preachers functioning in these positions? Are they really qualified for these leadership positions?

David Hester, in the article, "Practicing Governance in the Light of Faith," invites a discussion on who should serve on governing boards and in leadership positions of faith-based entities and whether or not their focus is, or should be, any different from sitting on the board of a secular entity.[2] The argument in the book is that the same focus, skills, talents, and professionalism needed by secular entities is needed in the leadership for the church to achieve its mission. Secular companies deal with issues of fund-raising, budgets, institutional policies, mission, goals, and maintenance and improvements of the facilities. These are the same topics discussed at most church meetings. Secular companies have varied individuals with varying talents, skills, and occupations as members of their boards or in leadership. If this is the case, why then is leadership in the church most often limited to licensed ministers?

Tradition, as supported by Mintzberg in his book, *Power In and Around Organizations*, is one of the potential reasons only licensed ministers served in positions of leadership previously. Although the focus of his book is not on churches, it does focus on the theory of management. In simple terms, churches have used licensed ministers because they traditionally were the only ones identified as having a call to work in the ministry and, as a result, were placed in positions in which they may not have been qualified.

Another potential reason why traditional Baptist churches use only licensed ministers is the lack of qualified persons willing to take the church positions. This is supported in "Hear the Words of the Wise," an article by John M. Montgomery in his book, *Money, Power, Greed: Has the Church Been Sold Out?*[3] In this article, Montgomery acknowledges and compares the church to the secular world of business, where "good top-level executives are very hard to come by." The secular world, he goes on to say, has nationwide searches for its leadership. The pool of applicants who are truly qualified, even with nationwide searches, is limited. In comparing this type of search to the church, Montgomery shows that in the church setting, the criteria for leadership make the pool of applicants even smaller. Within the church setting, a leader is required to be "born again, and have the same beliefs as the man at the top of the ministry." In addition, states Montgomery, if the "organization is Pentecostal, then all the leaders must be Pentecostal. If Lutheran, all must be Lutheran, and so on. A Southern Baptist organization is not inclined to heed the advice of Catholics; an Assembly of God will not seek the advice from the Lutherans."

Montgomery identifies this dilemma as a "mind-set" problem where qualified persons are not being fully utilized by various denominations and, instead, friends and relatives of leaders are allowed to be put into positions simply because they agree with the philosophy or doctrine of the denomination. Montgomery concludes by saying, "Leaders of great ministries can become greater by listening to the wise counsel of people who are experts in specific fields."

Few will argue that churches, for the most part, are not entrenched with traditions. Traditions can be positive and negative. The key is understanding which traditions need to cease because they hinder positive changes and which traditions need to remain because they are still effective.

The church of the new millennium is not limited by traditions or titles in filling the leadership roles. It has gone back to explore the foundation of biblical leadership and is embracing the essential elements for the existence of leadership as revealed in God's infallible plan. The issue is not tradition, individuals, or titles, but the call and gift of leadership bestowed by God on individuals to lead the church in the ultimate will of God for their ministry context.

So, what title should be given to those to fill the areas of leadership described above? Your guess is as good as mine. Even after all this discussion, it is a futile exercise to even try to begin to set universal titles for roles the leaders must walk in to further kingdom work. I hope by now you have come to the conclusion that a title ultimately means nothing until someone in authority—the leader—speaks to what the title means in your church setting.

Michael Miller, in *Kingdom Leadership*, sums up this area of discussion best when he says, "[A] kingdom leader can be defined as a person called by God to follow Christ in a life of discipleship, utilizing the leadership gifts given by the Holy Spirit to lead the church in carrying out the Great Commission for the purpose of expanding the kingdom of God."[4]

## CHAPTER 4

# I'VE BEEN CALLED...
# BUT TO DO WHAT?

T his is perhaps the most controversial discussion we can undertake. The issues are how one knows that someone has been called by God and for what purpose(s)? The Bible is clear that by the fruit one bears you will know them. Matthew 7:15–20 reads:

> Beware of false prophets who come disguised as harmless sheep, but are really wolves that will tear you apart. You can detect them by the way they act, just as you can identify a tree by its fruit. You don't pick grapes from thorn bushes, or figs from thistles. A healthy tree produces good fruit, and an unhealthy tree produces bad fruit. A good tree can't produce bad fruit, and a bad tree can't produce good fruit. So every tree that does not produce good fruit is chopped down and thrown into the fire. Yes, the way

to identify a tree or a person is by the kind of fruit that is produced.

Who should fill the positions identified as needed in the body of Christ? It is obvious that at least a licensed and ordained minister must fill one of the positions. That is normally the one who preaches, teaches, and casts the visions. The other positions should be filled with Kingdom individuals who have demonstrated their call to the ministry, and God's gifts and talents should be evident in filling the position to which they are being called through their lifestyles and fruits of the spirit.

Miller, in *Kingdom Leadership*, says there is a need for a high level of ministry competencies that includes skills required to accomplish the various ministry tasks of the Kingdom. What are the ministry tasks of the Kingdom? Ephesians 4:11–13 says:

> He is the one who gave these gifts to the church: the apostles, the prophets, the evangelists, and the pastors and teachers. Their responsibility is to equip God's people to do His work and build up the church, the body of Christ, until we come to such unity in our faith, and knowledge of Gods' Son that we will mature and full grown in the Lord, measuring up to the full stature of Christ.

Based on this scripture, God has identified individuals, whom He will hold accountable, to use their gifts to spiritually mature the members of the church. They are the prophets, evangelists, pastors, and teachers. These individuals should be, for discussion and thought purposes, the ultimate leaders of the church.

This is a good time to revisit a comment a well-known

national preacher once made on Jesus' selection process of the twelve disciples. He commented that when Jesus began his ministry, he "called"—or chose—twelve men. This was nothing new or exciting. However, what was revelatory in the explanation of Jesus' selection process was the fact that Jesus did not call twelve Pharisees, Sadducees, or elders that were already recognized as religious leaders. The preacher indicated Jesus called twelve businessmen. The disciples were a mix of commercial fishermen who had other men working for them, a tax collector, and a physician. The preacher indicated Jesus needed men who knew how to do business (had skills, talents, and gifting) because He could teach them how to pray.

Far too often in the church, we do not follow Jesus' example. We typically pick people who know how to pray but are clueless to ministry leadership. Where is it written that leaders must be individuals who have acknowledged a call to preach? If the individual has been called to "preach," let him or her preach. But for those who have been called to leadership, let them lead the people. An effective leader displays strength, skills, and fruitful traits.

J. Oswald Sanders was quoted as saying, "Leadership is the ability to organize the spiritual gifts and limitations of others."[1] Larry Gilbert was quoted as saying, "Building an effective team depends on putting the right people in the right place."[2] Both quotes support identifying the right people and empowering them for the right position.

It is time now for the church of the twenty-first century to teach there is more than one call from God to kingdom leadership. God is calling, now more than ever, those He has gifted to come forward and exercise their gifts in the church. Until the church begins to teach that there are different calls from God, those individuals who sense God's presence and call on their lives will continue to believe that God must be calling them to preach. This may not be the case. God may be calling them to teach, to lead administration, or to lead an evangelical movement. Do these calls mean that one must acknowledge a call from God as a preacher in order to be "set apart" for ministry?

In most Baptist churches, the only leaders set apart are preachers and deacons. Why is that? Shouldn't all kingdom leaders who have been called by God to lead the people be set apart? (We are not talking here about everyone who currently has a title as some type of leader or will hold a position for a certain amount of time.) God calls all kingdom leaders to leadership positions through the leader. We need only look to the Bible in Numbers 1:47–50 where there is a discussion on the role of the Levites. The Levites were those called by God to assist the priest (pastor) in the tabernacle. God then tells Moses to assign them to various levels of duties and responsibilities and to whom they reported (Num. 3:25–4:20). God instructed Moses that the Levites were to be anointed and set apart for their ministry (Num. 3:3). Being anointed and set apart before the people serve several purposes:

- The primary purpose is to pray for the person set apart and to offer him or her as a special offering to God for the work of the kingdom (Num. 8:13).

- Second, the people are given a clear message of any transfer of power and authority to the individual (Num. 8:10–11).

- Third, the people will know to whom to look for certain matters (Num. 8:14–15).

- Fourth, the people set apart are clear on what they are being held accountable to do (Num. 18:1).

All of these reasons line up with the essential elements of leadership as outlined earlier. Identifying and setting apart leadership is demonstrated throughout the Bible. When Moses asked God for a replacement to his leadership, God told Moses to lay his hands on Joshua, present him to the whole community and publicly commission him (Num. 27:18–20). When Joseph was appointed by Pharaoh to rule Egypt second only to Pharaoh himself, Pharaoh publicly acknowledged and empowered Joseph. He did this by giving Joseph a signet ring as a symbol of his authority; dressed him in beautiful clothing and put a royal chain about his neck; gave him the chariot normally reserved for the second in command, so that all who saw him pass knew of his authority; and finally, Pharaoh made explicit Joseph's authority by saying, "no one will move a hand or a foot in the entire land of Egypt without [his] approval" (Gen. 41:37–44).

Therefore, the church of the twenty-first century needs to think through its processes of setting apart individuals for ministry and what it really means. It is biblically grounded but needs to be used, as with titles, in your contextual environment.

## CHAPTER 5

# BE ACCOUNTABLE
# FOR YOUR ACTIONS

Hebrews 13:17 reminds us to "obey [our] spiritual leaders and do what they say. Their work is to watch over your souls, and they know they are accountable to God...." Many church leaders teach this passage to the members with regard to obeying them and what they say as a leader. There is nothing incorrect in that. However, many church leaders and pastors take the last part of this scripture out of context, or at a minimum, do not take the time to fully comprehend what God really meant by "accountability."

Many pastors and leaders, if you ask them who holds them accountable, will respond with "God." Failure of pastors to have human brothers and sisters of the faith hold them accountable for their actions has led to the downfall of many ministries.

# What's in a Title?

There are countless books on Christian leadership and many sermons that have been preached on the topics of pastors having covering, or being mentored, or having "fathers" in the ministry who will hold them accountable for their actions while leading a church. That is because pastors are discovering that they are still flesh, and their flesh was not saved when they became a leader. They need to know someone here on earth is watching over them and will "call them on the carpet" if the need arises.

Pastors (all leaders) need to be held accountable for their continued spiritual growth and maturity, financial stewardship, and family life. Far too often, pastors feel if they have graduated from a seminary, their educational days are over. This is far from the truth. Their educational experience is just beginning. Great leaders are life-long learners, according to renowned author and leader John Maxwell. Pastors, therefore, need someone who will challenge them to continue their learning process. They need to attend seminars and workshops, and take continuing education classes on leadership, management, and biblical studies.

Pastors also need to ensure their financial household is in order. 1 Timothy 3:5 raises the question of how one can manage the household of God if he cannot manage his or her own household. Whether we want to admit it or not, how one manages his or her own finances is directly related to how decisions will be made about the financial situations in God's house. Pastors need to be the first to exemplify generous giving of their finances to the ministry, to other worthy causes, and to individuals. Many pastors are not able to do this because their personal finances are a disgrace. Many have poor credit, unmanageable debt, and are one paycheck from filing bankruptcy just like the average

American. This leads the pastor to make decisions based on the monetary rewards—or lack thereof—rather than listening to what God desires for him or her to do with his or her finances. Needless to say, lack of finances has caused fear in pastors' ability to teach and preach the word of God for fear of being "fired" or "put out" of their church. Fear of being fired is a normal anxiety; however, pastors should not allow their financial situation to hold them hostage to any decision-making crisis.

Many pastors and leaders, unfortunately, do not feel they need to be continual learners in the areas of leadership, management, and finances. In a study by Daniel Conway, entitled, *Clergy as Reluctant Stewards of Congregational Resources,* the results indicated that clergy simply do not value financial management, stewardship, and leadership training while in school. The study was conducted by sending a 25- to 30-minute self-administered questionnaire to 211 accredited theological schools in the United States and Canada. The study goes on to say that only about half the clergy were satisfied with their *ability and skills* in administrative, financial, personnel, and strategic planning skills in comparison with more than 60 percent who were satisfied with their skills in areas of theological or pastoral responsibilities.[1] Many linked their lack of ability to not being taught such topics while attending seminary. The results further showed that many of the theological schools were not "uniformly supportive of the idea that seminaries *should* teach church leaders about leadership, stewardship, and management of church's resources."[2] Less than half of the clergy that responded indicated that they were even *interested* in these topics if even offered in seminary. Clergy do not value courses on management, leadership, and finances because seminaries do not value these courses as demonstrated by their lack of effort in adding these courses as anything other than elective courses; not mandatory.

Leadership skills, or lack thereof, are so critical to the success or failure of governance within the church. So many churches are expanding their ministries to include daycares, schools, assisted living facilities, independent senior living facilities, not to forget their regular worship services and outreach ministries. Many of these churches are using government grants or bank loans to assist in the purchase or building of these facilities. However, many churches fail to add new leadership in proportion to the increased need for additional skill sets to effectively operate these additional ministries. The current pastor is expected to handle not only the current responsibilities, but the added responsibilities that may require training and education in the areas of accounting, managing a large budget, controlling building programs in excess of millions of dollars, complex tax laws, etc. In most cases, the current pastor does not possess (nor does he want to possess according to the study) all the necessary skills and training to manage such enterprises and before long, the church realizes that poor decisions have been made regarding the affairs because of the lack of expertise at the leadership level.

The failure to put appropriate persons in positions of leadership is a leading cause of problems in the church as articulated by Sandra Hartman in *Organizational Structure in the Larger Church Setting: Emerging Issues*. She writes, "the church needs a taller structure (currently overly decentralized) and the use of a professional administrator...a true office manager...preferably someone with MBA-level experience and skills to handle the financial and administrative affairs."[3]

There has been extensive study and research on the lives of pastors and their families. It has been discovered that professional ministerial families are highly dysfunctional, and the divorce rate is extremely high. Tim Franklin, in his article, "Your Pastor Is Only Human," published by *Charisma*, details the stresses of a pastor's family living in a "fishbowl."[4] Pastors struggle with separating ministry of God from church work, which is never-ending. Examples can be found throughout the Bible of God's view of the sanctity of marriage. Marriage is to be treasured as a gift from God for a lifetime. Gifts from God are to be cared for, nurtured, and appreciated. Clearly the call to ministry is also for a lifetime; yet, the call to your current church may be but for the blink of an eye.

Pastors have regrettably sacrificed familial relationships and interactions such as attending their children's school and extracurricular activities or spending quality time with their spouses. In exchange, they have devoted countless hours to attending to the needs of their congregation, fostering short-term relationships only to be devastated when that same church member talks negatively about them or worse, leaves the church to join another one. Unfortunately, those valuable family moments can never be recaptured. Although their spouses may be there physically, pastors' spouses may emotionally detach from their mates when quality time is not devoted to maintaining and progressing the relationship. A troubled and dysfunctional family life does affect a pastor's ability to minister well before his or her congregation.

To assist a pastor with the lack of financial leadership and management skills as well as counseling for potential family concerns, every pastor needs a "covering." A covering is a person led to the pastor (or the pastor to them), by the Holy Spirit, whom the pastor will respect and will allow them to admonish, discipline, and guide the pastor toward accountability, if necessary. In essence, this is the person who will hold the pastor accountable for his spiritual growth, financial stewardship, and family life. Many pastors are being led by the Holy Spirit to select other pastors to be their covering. These are pastors whom they respect and believe God has connected them with in such a way that the covering has the anointed ability to speak to them with wisdom and guidance in their ministry journey.

In traditional churches, deacons believe it is their "call" to hold pastors accountable. This is difficult to do because the pastor has been sent to feed the deacons spiritually and to lead them. How then, can a deacon, as the covering, successfully hold the pastor accountable? Ideally, the covering has no vested interest in the church and therefore can be as objective as needed. The covering should not be affected by the lack of discipline that may be displayed by the pastor in the areas of spiritual maturity, financial stewardship, and family life. Usually, this is not the case for the deacons. Many times, not necessarily to their discredit, the deacons—because of their simultaneous relationships with the pastor and church—become disenchanted with the pastor because of the lack of discipline. In addition, the pastor may feel that the deacons' opinions of him or her will weaken if he or she is honest and display vulnerability. Deacons also may often have preconceived opinions, can easily be persuaded by family members and friends, or may have a biased interest in seeing the church move in a particular way that may hinder their ability to really hold the pastor accountable.

Churches and pastors are beginning to understand this

concept and are readily accepting the idea of pastors identifying a covering for accountability. The covering is normally not a member of the local pastor's church. Receiving guidance from an objective individual can be extremely vital in certain situations. The covering is usually:

- Someone who is well respected among his peers and his/her lifestyle is showing the good fruit of righteous living to be used as an example to follow

- Someone who moves in the same or similar circle as the pastor and will be in the "loop" to know what the pastor is doing or not doing

- Someone able to address moral issues, if needed, and to provide an unbiased plan for discipline along with a forum for restitution without the emotional attachment church members may have

- Someone who can provide spiritual growth either through workshops, seminars, or conferences so that the pastor can attend and be spiritually lifted and fed

- Someone the pastor can support with financial gifts and offerings. Galatians 6:6 reminds us that we should financially support those who spiritually enrich us. Your covering is praying for you and asking God to bless you. Your covering has your best interest at heart. Honor the covering. You reap what you sow. All of God's principles operate on

the principle of divine exchange. The covering is a divine exchange. The exchange must
be complete in order to be blessed by the
relationship

Whether the pastor chooses a covering is not what is most important. What is important is that pastors begin to understand that they need an earthly vessel to hold them accountable for their actions. Those truly called by God to the gospel ministry want to live a life that is pleasing to God. In the end, everyone wants to hear, "Well done, my good and faithful servant" (Matt. 25:21).

CHAPTER 6

# FOLLOW THE LEADER...
# IT'S NOT A GAME!

"Follow the leader" was a common childhood game. Many of you may be familiar with the game. One child was selected as the leader, and the other children cheerfully followed every command given by the leader without questioning. Children followed with blind obedience. If someone failed to do what the leader commanded, that person was immediately eliminated from the game. The objective of the game was to be the last person left who had followed all the commands correctly. If you were successful, you became the next leader.

The church of yesterday and the traditional churches of today follow the leader/pastor—as in the child's game—because of the respect for the title and/or position the person holds. Rarely are questions asked about decisions made for fear of being labeled a "troublemaker." Subordinate leaders are obedient, and all are awaiting their turn to be the next leader of the church or ministry group.

The 1980s and 1990s, however, brought about numerous public scandals and reports of mismanagement, immoral behavior, abuse of power, and financial misappropriations within the church leadership across sizes and denominations. As a result, feelings of distrust, hurt, and confusion emerged. There was a rush to change the organizational policies to prevent such reoccurrences. Subordinate leaders attempted to become the "accountable" council to the pastor. Although their motives may have been honorable, this type of "Monday morning quarterbacking" leadership style, in most cases, only stifled church growth and ministry. The well-meaning interference also closed the ears of the church to the Holy Spirit, who works through the leader/shepherd and not the membership/flock.

God, in His infinite wisdom and plan, chooses one person to be the shepherd of the flock. He allows the shepherd to select individuals to assist him/her in their leadership responsibilities. God chose Moses who then selected Aaron, Miriam, and a few others to assist him (Exodus 18:13–22). Even when a leader disappointed God, He did not change His method of selection. God chose a new leader. Joshua succeeded Moses, Elijah's mantle fell upon Elisha, and King David replaced King Saul. There is not an instance in the Bible where God went from one leader to a "group or committee" of individuals as the leader. 3 John 1:11 says, "Dear friend, don't let this bad example influence you. Follow only what is good. Remember that those who do good prove that they are God's children, and those who do evil prove that they do not know God." Unfortunately, there always will be bad apples in the barrel. However, those truly called to lead are subject to momentary falls as we are all human. This is when an effective covering can assist in restoring the leader to a right relationship with God.

Kingdom church leaders are not expecting members to blindly follow and never ask questions. The leaders are ready, equipped, and have studied the word of God in preparation to answer the tough questions about the decisions they make. They demand and deserve the respect and authority that comes with the position of leadership; however, they also realize they must live up to that level of respect and authority each and every day. These leaders are seeking and deserving to be surrounded by a "Joshua spirit."

If the cry of the church is for great leadership, then the cry of the leader must be for a Joshua. What is a Joshua spirit? A Joshua spirit ministers to the leader and helps them wherever they may need assistance. Who was Joshua? He was an assistant to Moses for many years before he ascended to leadership (Num. 11:28). It was Joshua, along with Caleb, who followed the orders of Moses to scout out the land. While the other ten scouts did not believe in the vision Moses articulated was from God, Joshua and Caleb believed in God and Moses as their leaders and were ready to move when Moses gave the command (Num. 13:25–30). Joshua was the one ready to go to battle on the front lines (Exod. 17:9–13) while Moses stood on the mountaintop during the battle to encourage the troops. How many times do church members perceive this as the pastor trying to "stay clean" or acting "too good to do the dirty work" when in reality, the leader is doing exactly what his or her role calls for at that point in time.

Joshua waited more than forty years before he became the leader. During those forty years, he ministered to the needs of Moses. Today we would consider Moses to be Joshua's mentor. Joshua gleaned wisdom and learning by submitting to Moses' leadership and giving honor and respect to his leader.

Hebrews 13:17 reminds us once again to "obey your spiritual leaders and do what they say. Their work is to watch over your souls, and they know they are accountable to God. Give them reason to do this joyfully and not with sorrow. That would certainly not be for your benefit." How many times has that scripture been read? Attention needs to be given to the last statement that is so often overlooked. It is saying that it would not be to our benefit to disobey the leader.

There is no doubt Joshua's blessings came out of obedience to the leadership of Moses. Joshua did not obey Moses because he was expecting a blessing—like so many church members are—but because of his love for God and his understanding of how God works through the leader. In the end, Joshua was given the role of leader and was blessed with an inheritance of land and many material goods. One must also be reminded here that "You will always reap what you sow!" (Gal. 6:7). When Joshua became the leader, he reaped what he had sown. He had great followers that made leading the people of Israel a blessing rather than a curse. Joshua and the people of Israel experienced great successes. Terry Nance, in his book, *God's Armor Bearer: How to Serve God's Leaders*, says, "The unity between a leader and his staff is in the spirit and not by the blood."[1] He emphasizes that God will send you quality people to help you carry out your mission if you pray to him. God may send help through your family and/or non-family members. The point made is that the leader and the followers must be of the same spirit in order to work together. "Can two walk together, unless they are agreed?" is a common quote from the Bible (Amos 3:3, NKJV).

Leaders need good followers; and followers need good leaders. Nance goes on to say in the same book, "that whether a follower sees the leader do great things, or make great mistakes, the follower must still remain faithful to him."[2] Nance says every leader has at least four faces:

- The lion
- The calf
- The man
- The eagle

The leader is a "lion" when it comes to dealing with a problem, "calf" when it comes to serving people, "man" when it comes to tending the sheep and "eagle" when it comes to standing up to minister the Word of God. But you will also see your leader as a human being when he or she is hurt and wounded. Most followers only want to see their leader as an eagle. It is easy to respect the leader when he or she is acting as an eagle under God's anointing. But you must also show respect when times are hard and he or she is operating more as a man or woman. The leader is entitled to respect.

Respect must be reciprocal among followers and leaders. Leaders must be willing to invest the time in the followers, just as Elijah did Elisha and Moses did Joshua, to nurture and develop them into leaders so they are ready to answer the call from God when the time comes.

Together, leader and followers can accomplish much for the kingdom. The time has come to stop the infighting among the leadership about who is in charge. God is in charge. The church and its ministry belong to God. Let the Holy Spirit rule. The Bible is clear on how God establishes His plan through His chosen leader. God will send people to help you carry the load of ministry.

Are you praying for a double anointing to fall on you as it did Elisha? Then honor the leader God has put in your life to lead and teach you, just as Elisha did unto Elijah. The followers of today are the leaders of tomorrow.

Leaders... follow God. Followers... follow the leader... it's not a game!

# COMPARISON OF CHURCH TITLES TO SECULAR COUNTERPARTS

| Church | Secular |
|---|---|
| Senior Pastor | Board/Chair/President |
| Executive Pastor | Chief Executive Officer |
| Minister of Pastoral Care | Chief Operating Officer |
| Financial Secretary | Controller |
| Associate Ministers | Vice Presidents |
| Ministry leaders | Department Heads |

# Questions for Group Discussion

## Chapter 1:
## Leadership Is a Calling and a Gift From God

1. Name other biblical reasons for why leadership structure was created.

2. Can you name scripture or examples that support abilities of leadership at birth and leadership through experience?

3. What does it mean to you to be "under" leadership authority in your church?

4. Do you honor your leader?

5. How do you revere your leader?

6. How do you respect your leader?

7. How do you pay tribute to your leader?

8. How do you hold them in great admiration?

## Chapter 2:
## What's in a Title?

1. What titles confuse you as a church member?

2. List traditions in your church that you do not consider biblically grounded. List those traditions that you do consider biblically grounded. Why or why not?

3. What traditions are no longer effective in your church? Why?

4. What traditions are still effective in your church? Why?

## Chapter 3:
## Leaders Are Not Defined by Their Titles

1. List the leaders and their titles in your church. What are their responsibilities, who holds them accountable, and to whom do they report?

2. What is your current leadership model? (Draw the model if it is easier.) Does it line up with the essential elements of leadership? Why or why not?

3. Do you agree or disagree with David Hester with regard to secular companies being very similar to churches and with respect to issues to be discussed, handled, and decisions made?

## Chapter 4:
## I've Been Called... But to Do What?

1. How do you select your leaders? Appointed, nominated, or other?

2. Are all your leaders licensed ministers of the gospel?

3. What positions are "set apart" as leadership? Do you think this is enough or should other positions be set apart? Why or why not?

## Chapter 5:
## Be Accountable for Your Actions

1. What leaders are currently set apart in your church? Why? Do you think it should change?

2. What do you think about coverings? Are they similar to anything that already exists in your church?

3. What do you think about council of elders? Is it similar to anything that already exists in your church?

4. Does your pastor have a covering? If not, who holds your pastor accountable? Do you still agree with this approach?

# CASE STUDY

$N$ote: The current debate between Schools of Theology and alumni of these schools is the lack of training and/or classes in leadership, management of churches, and financial stewardship. Research shows most pastors feel ill-equipped or inexperienced to teach such subjects. Schools of Theology are reluctant to hire anyone other than preachers/pastors to teach in their schools. This dilemma is not unlike churches that are reluctant to hire anyone other than licensed ministers.

**Using the information below, begin a dialogue on the questions that follow.**

An individual has more than twenty years of experience in corporate America working and supervising individuals in money management, payroll, accounts payable, investments, and other duties normally associated with a corporate controller. The individual is also a Certified Public Accountant, has worked in public accounting, and has even had his own CPA firm. The individual has also taught Accounting at a university for five years in the School of Business. The individual has an earned doctorate degree from a well-respected school of management. Finally, the individual has been active in the life of a local church for more than twenty years and has done extensive work with churches in the areas of leadership, finance, and administration of all denominations and cultures both nationally and internationally.

**For discussion and thought:**

- Is this individual qualified to teach Church Administration and Finance in a School of Theology? Why or why not?

- If this same individual acknowledges a call from God to the Gospel ministry and becomes licensed (without furthering any educational requirements), is this individual now qualified to teach Church Finance and Administration at a School of Theology? Why or why not?

- Is a preacher/pastor without any experience other than as pastor of a congregation better able to teach Church Administration and Finance at a School of Theology?

**Group dialogue on the above case study is encouraged to be sent to:**

Keys to the Kingdom
P.O. Box 1332
Chesapeake, Va. 23327
Or send an e-mail to the author at
Valerie.Brown@Mt-Lebanon.org

# ABOUT THE AUTHOR

Elder Valerie K. Brown is a native of Chesapeake, Va. Elder Brown readily serves beside her husband, the Rev. Dr. Kim Walter Brown, Senior Pastor of Mount Lebanon Missionary Baptist Church, also in Chesapeake. She serves as the Executive Pastor. Together they are the proud parents of two children, James and Kimberly.

Elder Brown has an earned doctorate degree in Business Management from The Weatherhead School of Management, Case Western Reserve University, Cleveland, Ohio. Dr. Brown received her CPA certification in 1980 in the State of Virginia and is an Associate Professor of Management at the Samuel D. Proctor School of Theology, Virginia Union University, Richmond, Va., where she teaches Church Administration, Finance, and Leadership in the Masters of Divinity Program.

# Notes

## Preface

1. Henry Mintzberg, *Power In and Around Organizations* (Upper Saddle River, NJ: Prentice Hall, 1983), 153.

2. Paul Salipante and Karen Golden-Biddle, *Managing Traditionality and Strategic Change in Nonprofit Organizations* (Indianapolis, IN: Jossey-Bass Publishers, 1995).

## Chapter 3
### Leaders Are Not Defined by Their Titles

1. Phillip V. Lewis, *Transformational Leadership: A New Model for Total Church Involvement* (Nashville, TN: Broadman & Holman, 1996).

2. David Hester, "Practicing Governance in the Light of Faith," in *Building Effective Boards for Religious Organizations*, ed. by Thomas Holland and David Hester (Indianapolis, IN: Jossey-Bass, 2000) 58–79.

3. John M. Montgomery, *Money, Power, Greed: Has the Church Been Sold Out?* (Ventura, CA: Regal Books, 1987).

4. Michael Miller, *Kingdom Leadership* (n.p.: Religious Activities Press, 1996).

### CHAPTER 4
### I'VE BEEN CALLED ... BUT TO DO WHAT?

1. J. Oswald Sanders, *Spiritual Leadership* (Chicago, IL: Moody Press, 1994), 137.

2. Larry Gilbert and Cindy Spear, *The Big Book of Job Descriptions for Ministry* (Ventura, CA: Gospel Light, 2002).


### CHAPTER 5
### BE ACCOUNTABLE FOR YOUR ACTIONS

1. Daniel Conway, "Clergy as Reluctant Stewards of Congregational Resources," *Financing American Religion* (Lanham, MD: Altamira Press, 1998), 97–98.

2. Ibid., 100

3. Sandra Hartman, "Organizational Structure in the Larger Church Setting: Emerging Issues," *Journal of Ministry Marketing and Management*, 1997, 54-55.

4. Tim Franklin, "Your Pastor Is Only Human," *Charisma,* May 2001.


### CHAPTER 6
### FOLLOW THE LEADER ... IT'S NOT A GAME!

1. Terry Nance, *God's Armor Bearer: How to Serve God's Leaders* (Shippensburg, PA: Destiny Image, 2003).

2. Ibid.